D0578700

Published by Simple Truths, LLC. 1952 McDowell Road,
Suite 300, Naperville, Illinois 60563

Simple Truths is a registered trademark.

Printed and bound in the United States of America.
ISBN: 978-1-60810-162-7

www.simpletruths.com
Toll Free 800-900-3427

Book Design: Brian Frantz - Simple Truths

Photos provided by Shutterstock.com

01 WOZ 12

Christmas 2015

Achieve Any GOAL

12 Steps to Realizing Your Dreams

Jacob- Believe + Achieve! ♥ you, ashley

by Brian Tracy

Table of Contents

Introduction

Get Started: Unlock Your Potential

This is a wonderful time to be alive. There are almost unlimited opportunities today for creative and determined people to achieve more of their goals than ever before.

It's Not Where You Start- It's How You Finish

When I was eighteen, I left high school without graduating. My first job was as a dishwasher in the back of a small hotel. From there, I moved on to washing cars and then washing floors with a janitorial service. For the next few years, I drifted and worked at various laboring jobs, earning my living by the sweat of my brow. I worked in sawmills and factories. I worked on farms and ranches. I worked in the tall timber with a chain saw and dug wells when the logging season ended.

I worked as a construction laborer on tall buildings and as a seaman on a Norwegian freighter in the North Atlantic. Often I slept in my car or in cheap rooming houses. When I was twenty-three, I worked as an itinerant farm laborer during the harvest, sleeping on the hay in the farmer's barn and eating with the farmer's family. I was uneducated and unskilled, and at the end of the harvest, I was unemployed once more.

When I could no longer find a laboring job, I got a job in straight commission sales, cold-calling office-to-office and door-to-door. I would often work all day long to make a single sale so that I could pay for my rooming house and have a place to sleep that night. This was not a great start at life.

The Day My Life Changed

Then one day, I took out a piece of paper and wrote down an outrageous goal for myself. It was to earn $1,000 per month in door-to-door and office-to-office selling. I folded up the piece of paper, put it away, and never found it again.

But thirty days later, my entire life had changed. During that time, I discovered a technique for closing sales that tripled my income from the very first day. Meanwhile, the owner of my company sold out to an entrepreneur who had just moved into town. Exactly thirty days after I had written down my goal, the new owner took me aside and offered me $1,000 per month to head up the sales force and teach the other salespeople what I was doing that enabled me to sell so much more than anyone else. I accepted his offer, and from that day forward, my life was never the same.

Within eighteen months, I had moved from that job to another and then to another. I went from personal selling to becoming a sales manager with people selling for me. In a new business, I recruited and built a ninety-five-person sales force. I went literally from worrying about my next meal to walking around with a pocket full of $20 bills.

"Goals allow you to control the direction of change in your favor."
Brian Tracy

I began teaching my salespeople how to write out their goals and how to sell more effectively. In almost no time at all, they increased their incomes as much as tenfold. Today, many of them are millionaires and multimillionaires.

Life Goes Up and Down

I have to admit that since those days in my mid-twenties, my life has not been a smooth series of upward steps. It has included many ups and downs, marked by occasional successes and temporary failures. I have traveled, lived, and worked in more than ninety countries, learning French, German, and Spanish along the way and working in twenty-two different fields.

As the result of inexperience and sometimes sheer stupidity, I have spent or lost everything I made and had to start over again—several times. Whenever this happened, I would begin by sitting down with a piece of paper and laying out a new set of goals for myself, using the methods that I'll explain in the pages ahead.

After several years of hit-and-miss goal setting and goal achieving, I finally decided to collect everything I had learned into a single system. By assembling these ideas and strategies in one place, I developed a goal-setting methodology and process, with a beginning, middle, and end, and began to follow it every day.

Within one year, my life had changed once more. In January of that year, I was living in a rented apartment with rented furniture. I was $35,000 in debt and driving a used car that wasn't paid for. By December, I was living in my own $100,000 condominium. I owned a new Mercedes, had paid off all my debts, and had $50,000 in the bank.

Then I really got serious about success. I realized that goal setting was incredibly powerful. I invested hundreds and then thousands of hours reading and researching goal setting and goal achieving, synthesizing the best ideas I could find into a complete process that worked with incredible effectiveness.

Anyone Can Do It

Some years later, I began audiotaping and videotaping my workshops and seminars so that others could use them. We have now trained hundreds of thousands of people in these principles, in multiple languages, all over the world.

What I found was that these ideas work everywhere, for everyone, in virtually every country, no matter what your education, experience, or background may be when you begin.

"Goals in writing
are dreams
with deadlines."
Brian Tracy

Best of all, these ideas have made it possible for me and many thousands of others to take complete control over our lives. The regular and systematic practice of goal setting has taken us from poverty to prosperity, from frustration to fulfillment, from underachievement to success and satisfaction. This system will do the same for you.

Create Your Own World

Perhaps the greatest discovery in human history is the power of your mind to create almost every aspect of your life.

Everything you see around you in the man-made world began as a thought or an idea in the mind of a single person before it was translated into reality. Everything in your life started as a thought, a wish, a hope, or a dream, either in your mind or in the mind of someone else. Your thoughts are creative. Your thoughts form and shape your world and everything that happens to you.

The great summary statement of all religions, philosophies, metaphysics, psychology, and success is this: *You become what you think about most of the time.* Your outer world ultimately becomes a reflection of your inner world. Your outer world of experience mirrors back to you what you think about most of the time. Whatever you think about continuously emerges in your reality.

Many thousands of successful people have been asked what they think about most of the time. The most common answer given by successful people is that they think about *what they want*—and *how to get it*—most of the time.

Unsuccessful, unhappy people think and talk about what they *don't want* most of the time. They talk about their problems and worries and who is to blame for their situation most of the time. But successful people keep their thoughts and conversations focused on their most intensely desired goals. They think and talk about what they want most of the time.

Living without clear goals is like driving in a thick fog. No matter how powerful or well engineered your car, you drive slowly, hesitantly, making little progress on even the smoothest road. Deciding upon your goals clears the fog immediately and allows you to focus and channel your energies and abilities toward what you really want. Clear goals enable you to step on the accelerator of your own life and race ahead rapidly toward achieving more of what you want in life.

Your Automatic Goal-Seeking Function

Imagine this exercise: You take a homing pigeon out of its roost, put it in a cage, cover the cage with a blanket, put the cage in a box, and then place the box into a closed truck cab. You can then drive a thousand miles in any direction. If you then open the truck cab, take out the box, take off the blanket, and let the homing pigeon out of the cage, the homing pigeon will fly up into the air, circle three times, and then fly unerringly back to its home roost a thousand miles away. No other creature on earth has this incredible cybernetic, goal-seeking function—except for *you*.

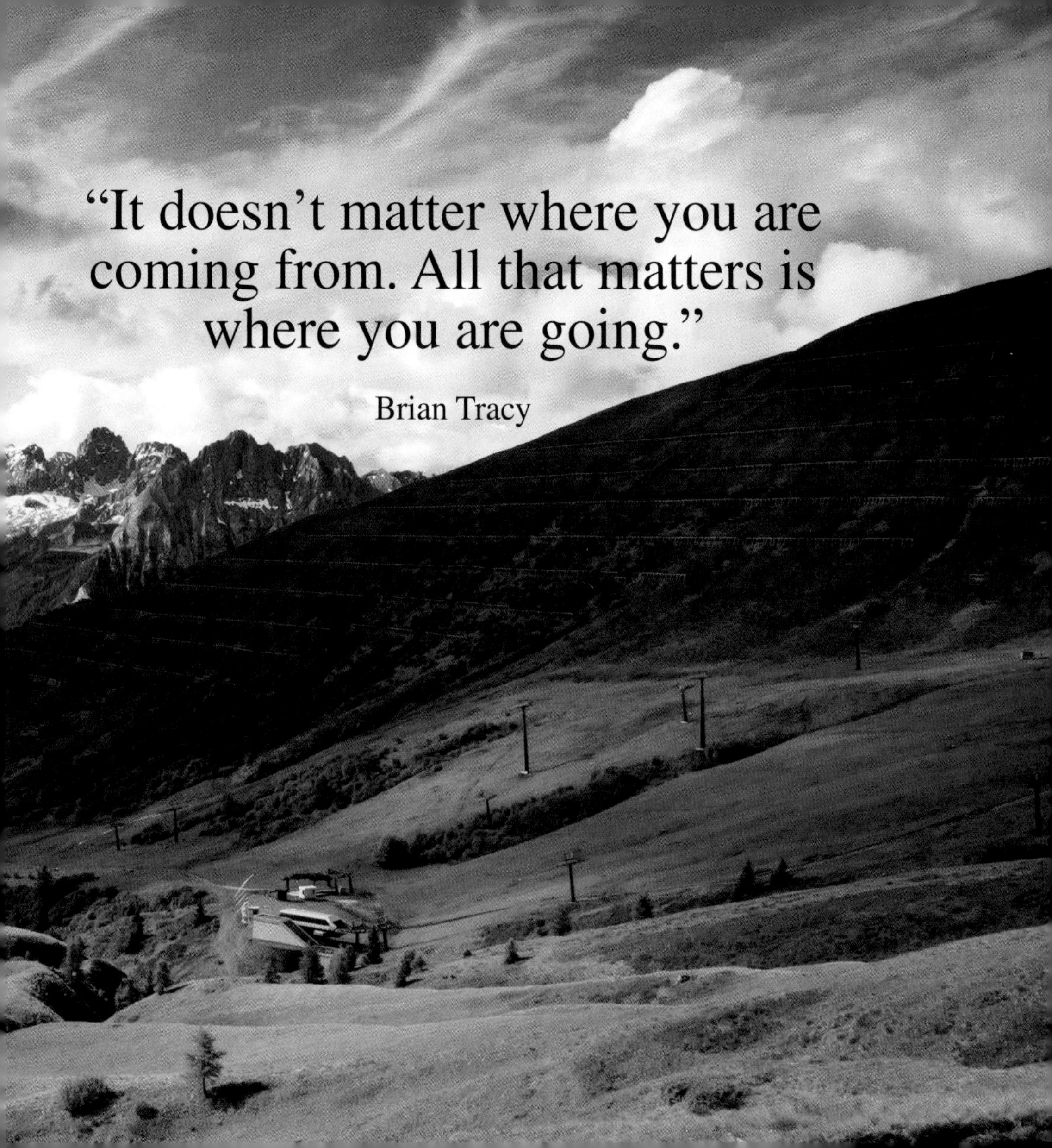
"It doesn't matter where you are coming from. All that matters is where you are going."
Brian Tracy

You have the same goal-achieving ability as the homing pigeon but with one marvelous addition. When you are absolutely clear about your goal, you do not even have to know how to achieve it. By simply deciding exactly what you want, you will begin to move unerringly toward your goal, and your goal will start to move unerringly toward you. At exactly the right time and in exactly the right place, you and the goal will meet.

Because of this incredible cybernetic mechanism located deep within your mind, you almost always achieve your goals, whatever they are.

Nature doesn't care about the size of your goals. If you set little goals, your automatic goal-achieving mechanism will enable you to achieve little goals. If you set large goals, this natural capability will enable you to achieve large goals. The size, scope, and detail of the goals you choose to think about most of the time are completely up to you.

Join the Top 3 Percent

Mark McCormack, in his book *What They Don't Teach You at Harvard Business School*, tells of a Harvard study conducted between 1979 and 1989. In 1979, the graduates of the MBA program at Harvard were asked, "Have you set clear, written goals for your future and made plans to accomplish them?"

It turned out that only 3 percent of the graduates had written goals and plans. Thirteen percent had goals, but they were not in writing. Fully 84 percent had no specific goals at all, aside from getting out of school and enjoying the summer.

Ten years later, in 1989, the researchers interviewed the members of that class again. They found that the 13 percent who had goals that were not in writing were earning, on average, *twice* as much as the 84 percent of students who had no goals at all. But most surprisingly, they found that the 3 percent of graduates who had clear, written goals when they left Harvard were earning, on average, *ten times* as much as the other 97 percent of graduates all together. The only difference between the groups was the clarity of the goals they had for themselves when they graduated.

Happiness Requires Goals

Goals give you that sense of meaning and purpose, a clear sense of direction. As you move toward your goals you feel happier and stronger. You feel more energized and effective.

You feel more competent and confident in yourself and your abilities. Every step you take toward your goals increases your belief that you can set and achieve even bigger goals in the future.

More people today fear change and worry about the future than at any other time in our history. One of the great benefits of goal setting is that goals enable you to control the direction of change in your life. Goals enable you to ensure that the changes in your life are largely self-determined and self-directed. Goals enable you to instill meaning and purpose into everything you do.

The great questions then become:
What are your goals?
What purposes are you aiming at?
Where do you want to end up at the end of the day?

You Hold The Key

Setting goals, working toward them day by day, and ultimately achieving them is the key to happiness in life. Goal setting is so powerful that the very act of thinking about your goals makes you happy, even before you have taken the first step toward achieving them.

To unlock and unleash your full potential, you should make a habit of daily goal setting and achieving for the rest of your life. You should develop a laser-like focus so that you are always thinking and talking about what you want rather than what you don't want. You must resolve, from this moment forward, to become a goal-seeking organism, like a guided missile or a homing pigeon, moving unerringly toward the goals that are important to you.

There is no greater guarantee of a long, happy, healthy, and prosperous life than for you to be continually working on being, having, and achieving more and more of the things you really want. Clear goals enable you to release your full potential for personal and professional success. Goals enable you to overcome any obstacle and to make your future achievements unlimited.

"If what you are doing is not moving you towards your goals, then it's moving you away from your goals."
Brian Tracy

Here is the twelve-step goal-setting methodology
that I have taught to more than a million people.
Depending upon your situation
and your particular needs,
you can vary these ingredients to create
the kind of goals and life
that you desire.

TWELVE STEPS

TO SET AND ACHIEVE ANY GOAL

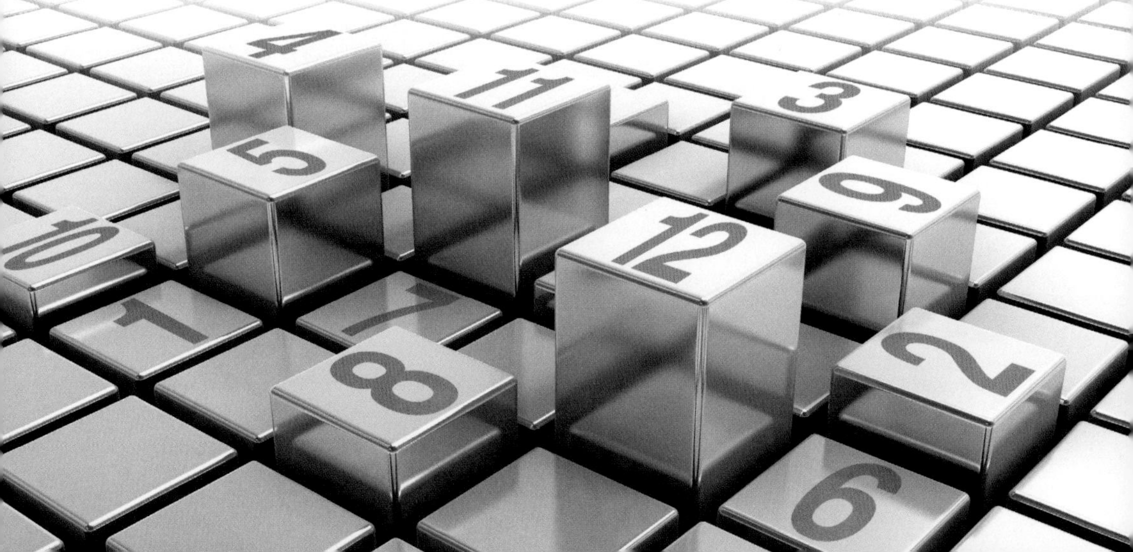

I

Have a Desire:

What Do You Really Want?

Stephen Covey once said, “Be sure that, as you scramble up the ladder of success, it is leaning against the right building.” Many people work hard to achieve goals that they think they want only to find, at the end of the day, that they get no joy or satisfaction from their accomplishments. They ask, “Is this all there is?” This occurs when the outer accomplishment is not in harmony with their inner values. Don’t let this happen to you.

Step number one in goal setting is to have a desire. You must have an intense, burning desire for your particular goal. This desire must be personal, something that you want for yourself. You can never want goals for someone else, nor can you get excited about a goal that someone else wants for you.

The great question you must eventually ask and answer is, *What do I really want to do in my life?* What do you really want for yourself in your heart of hearts? What would you be most excited or enthusiastic about achieving personally? If you could accomplish only one goal in the whole world and you were absolutely guaranteed success at that one goal, what one goal would it be? The intensity of your personal desire will determine the amount of energy and determination you put behind any goal you set for yourself.

Your major definite purpose can be defined as the one goal that is most important to you at the moment. It is usually the one goal that will help you to achieve more of your other goals than anything else you can accomplish. It must have the following characteristics:

1. It must be something that you *personally really want.* Your desire for this goal must be so intense that the very idea of achieving your major definite purpose excites you and makes you happy.

2. It must be *clear and specific*. You must be able to define it in words. You must be able to write it down with such clarity that a child could read it and know exactly what it is that you want and be able to determine whether or not you have achieved it.

3. It must be *measurable and quantifiable*. Rather than "I want to make a lot of money," it must be more like "I will earn $100,000 per year by (a specific date)."

4. It must be both *believable and achievable*. Your major definite purpose cannot be so big or so ridiculous that it is completely unattainable.

5. Your major definite purpose should have a *reasonable probability of success*, perhaps fifty-fifty when you begin. If you have never achieved a major goal before, set a goal that has an 80 percent or 90 percent probability of success. Make it easy on yourself, at least at the beginning. Later on, you can set huge goals with very small probabilities of success and you will still be motivated to take the steps necessary to achieve them. But in the beginning, set goals that are believable and achievable and that have a high probability of success so that you can be assured of winning right from the start.

6. Your major definite purpose must be *in harmony with your other goals*. Your major goals must be in harmony with your minor goals and congruent with your values.

Watch Your Behavior

How can you tell what your values really are? The answer is simple. You always demonstrate your true values in your actions, and especially your actions under pressure. Whenever you are forced to choose between one behavior and another, you will always act consistent with what is most important and valuable to you at that moment.

Values, in fact, are organized in a hierarchy. You have a series of values, some of them very intense and important and some of them weaker and less important. One of the most important exercises you can engage in to determine who you really are and what you really want, is to organize your values by *priority*. Once you are clear about the relative importance of your values, you can then organize your outer life so that it is in alignment with them.

Think About Your Goal

Your selection of a major definite purpose and your decision to concentrate single-mindedly on that purpose—overcoming all obstacles and difficulties until it is achieved—will do more to change your life for the better than any other decision you ever make. Whatever your major definite purpose, write it down and begin working on it today.

2

Believe That Your Goal Is Achievable

The second step in goal setting is to believe or have a conviction. You must absolutely believe, deep in your heart, that you deserve the goal and that you are capable of attaining it. Belief is the catalyst that activates all your mental and physical powers. Spiritually, we refer to belief as faith. All high achievers, in every field, are men and women of tremendous faith and conviction. They intensely believe in their ability to accomplish the goals they have set for themselves.

Wonderfully enough, when you set a clear goal for yourself—something that you really, really want—and you begin working toward it, day by day, you intensify your desire and deepen your belief. Every step forward deepens your conviction that it is possible for you.

Your level of confidence in your ultimate ability to succeed is the key determinant of your determination and persistence. It is therefore essential that you make your goals both believable and achievable, especially at the beginning.

For example, you cannot set a goal to go from poverty to financial independence within one year. This kind of a goal is self-defeating because it is so far beyond your capabilities. You must set a goal that is reachable, and then set another goal after that and another after that. By achieving small goals, one at a time, you build your self-confidence.

You develop forward momentum. You eventually reach the point where you become convinced that there is no goal that you cannot attain if you are clear about it and if you work at it long enough and hard enough. But you have to walk before you run when setting goals.

Change Your Thinking, Change Your Life

All improvement in your life comes from changing your beliefs about yourself and your possibilities. Would you like to double your income? Of course you would! Here is the question: Do you believe that it is possible? How would you like to triple your income? Do you believe that is possible as well? Whatever your level of skepticism, let me ask you a question. Since you started your first job, haven't you already doubled or tripled your income? Aren't you already earning vastly more than you earned when you started? Haven't you already proven to yourself that it is possible to double and triple your income? And what you have done before, you can do again—probably over and over—if you just learn how. You simply must believe that it is possible. Napoleon Hill said, **"Whatever the mind of man can conceive and believe, it can achieve."**

Garbage In, Garbage Out

Here is an interesting discovery about self-concept. Even if your self-concept is made up of erroneous beliefs about yourself or your world, as far as you are concerned these are *facts* and you will think, feel, and act accordingly.

As it happens, your beliefs about yourself are largely subjective. They are often not based on fact at all. They are the result of information you have taken in throughout your life and the way you have processed that information. Your beliefs have been shaped and formed by your early childhood, your friends and associates, your reading and education, your experiences—both positive and negative—and a thousand other factors. The worst of all beliefs are *self-limiting beliefs*. If you believe yourself to be limited in some way, whether or not it is true, it becomes true for you. If you believe it, you will act as if you were deficient in that particular area of talent or skill.

Overcoming self-limiting beliefs and self-imposed limitations is often the biggest obstacle standing between you and the realization of your full potential.

Select the Beliefs You Want

Imagine that there was a "Belief Store," very much like a computer software store, where you could purchase a belief to program into your subconscious mind. If you could choose any set of beliefs at all, which beliefs would be the most helpful to you?

Here is my suggestion. Select this belief: "I am destined to be a big success in life."

If you absolutely believe that you are destined to be a big success, you will walk, talk, and act as if everything that happens to you in life is part of a great plan to make you successful. And as it happens, this is how the top people think in every field.

Act Your Way into Feeling

The Law of Reversibility in psychology and metaphysics says, "You are more likely to act yourself into feeling a particular way than you are to feel yourself into acting."

What this means is that when you start, you may not feel like the great success that you desire to be. You will not have the self-confidence that comes from a record of successful achievement. You will often doubt your own abilities and fear failure. You will feel that you are not good enough, at least not yet.

But if you "act as if " you were already the person you desire to be, with the qualities and talents that you desire to have, your actions will generate the feelings that go with them. You will actually act yourself into feeling the way you want to feel by the Law of Reversibility.

If you want to be one of the top people in your business, dress like the top people. Groom yourself like the top people. Organize your work habits the way they do. Pick the most successful people in your field and use them as your role models. If possible, go to them and ask them for advice on how to get ahead more rapidly. And whatever advice they give you, follow it immediately. Take action.

When you start to walk, talk, dress, and behave like the top people, you soon will begin to *feel* like the top people. You will treat other people like the top people do. You will work the way the top people work. You will start to get the results that the top people get. In no time at all, you will be one of the top people yourself. It may be trite to say, "Fake it until you make it!" but there is a lot of truth to it.

Keep Your Words and Actions Consistent

Your beliefs are always manifested in your words and actions. Make sure that everything you say and do from now on is consistent with the beliefs that you want to have and the person that you want to become. In time, you will replace more and more of your self-limiting beliefs with life-enhancing beliefs. Over time, you will completely reprogram yourself for success. When this occurs, the transformation that takes place in your outer life will amaze you and all the people around you.

3

Write Your Goal Down

The third step to goal achievement is for you to write it down. A goal that is not in writing is not a goal at all. Everyone who succeeds greatly works from clear, written, specific, detailed goals and plans, reviewed regularly, sometimes every day. I personally recommend that you write and rewrite your goals each day, day after day, week after week, and month after month. This programs them deep into your subconscious mind where they take on a life and power of their own.

Continually ask yourself, "How will I measure success in the achievement of this goal? What standards will I create? What benchmarks or scorecards can I use to measure my progress?"

The act of writing is a psychoneuromotor activity. This means that when you write down a goal of any kind, you activate your emotions, your intelligence, and your physical body. Writing a goal down with a pen and paper activates your visual, auditory and kinesthetic senses. Writing the goal down on paper programs the goal into your subconscious mind, where it takes on a life of its own, working away twenty-four hours per day.

For example, if you were going to apply this approach to improving your relationships, you would write out a clear, present-tense, positive personal description of your ideal life and lifestyle in detail, exactly as if it were *already* perfect in every way. List each of the important people in your family and relationships, and then describe how your relationships with those people would look and feel like if they were perfect in every way.

Describe your ideal lifestyle. What would your life be like, from morning to evening, from Monday to Sunday, from January to December? If you were living your perfect lifestyle along with your family, what would you do together? How would you spend your time in the evenings, on the weekends and on vacations? Where would you go? What would you do when you got there?

Imagine no limitations. If your life were perfect, where would you live? What kind of a home would you have? What kind of material possessions would you want to provide for your family? What schools would you want your children to attend? What colleges would you want them to be able to afford? And what would you do to make this possible? What kind of clothes, cars, and possessions would you want to make available to the members of your family?

The very act of writing down
these factors on paper
increases your likelihood
of achieving them.

4

Determine Your Starting Point

The fourth step is for you to analyze your starting point in the attainment of your major goal or goals. Where are you now? If you want to lose weight, the very first thing you do is to weigh yourself to determine your baseline or current weight.

If you want to achieve a certain level of financial worth, you put together a personal financial statement for yourself and determine how much you are worth today.

When you assess your situation by analyzing your starting point, you are forced to be honest with yourself. This enables you to set goals that are believable and achievable rather than setting goals that may be unattainable and self-defeating.

Practice The Reality Principle

Jack Welch, CEO of General Electric for many years, once said that the most important quality of leadership is the "reality principle." He defined this as the ability to see the world as it really is, not as you wish it were. He would begin every meeting to discuss a goal or a problem with the question, "What's the reality?" Peter Drucker referred to this quality as "intellectual honesty," dealing with the facts exactly as they are before attempting to solve a problem or make a decision. Abraham Maslow once wrote that the first quality of the self-actualizing person was the ability to be completely honest and objective with himself or herself. It is the same with you.

If you want to be the best you can be and achieve what is truly possible for you, **you must be brutally honest with yourself about your point of departure.** You must sit down and analyze yourself in detail to decide exactly where you are today in each area.

Practice Zero-Based Thinking

When you begin to plan your long-term future, one of the most valuable exercises you can engage in is "zero-based thinking." In zero-based thinking, you ask this question: "Knowing what I now know, is there anything that I am doing today that I wouldn't start again if I had to do it over?" No matter who you are or what you are doing, there are activities and relationships in your life that, knowing what you now know, you wouldn't get involved in.

It is difficult, if not impossible, for you to make progress in your life if you allow yourself to be held back by decisions you made in the past. If there is something in your life that you wouldn't get into again today, your next question is, *How can I get out, and how fast?*

Imagine Starting Over

When you embark on the achievement of any great goal, you should imagine that at any time you could start over again. Never allow yourself to feel locked in or trapped by a particular decision from the past. Keep focused on the future.

Many people today are walking away from their educations, their businesses, their industries, and their years of experience and starting something completely new and different. They are honest enough to recognize that there is a limited future in what they are doing, and they are determined to try something where the future possibilities are far greater. You must do the same.

In doing a baseline assessment of yourself and your life, you must face the facts, whatever they are. As Harold Geneen of ITT once said, "Facts don't lie." Seek out the real facts, not the obvious facts, the apparent facts, the hoped-for facts, or the wished-for facts. The true facts are what you need to make good decisions.

Put Together Your Own Stratgic Plan

There is an old saying, "Well begun is half done." Doctors say, "Accurate diagnosis is half the cure." Taking the time to honestly evaluate each part of your situation before you launch toward your goal will save you months and even years on your journey. In many cases, it will force you to reevaluate your goals in the light of superior analysis and knowledge. It will dramatically improve the speed at which you achieve your goals once you get going.

5

Determine Why You Want It

The fifth step is for you to decide why you want a particular goal in the first place. Make a list of all the ways that you will personally benefit by achieving that goal. The more reasons you have for wanting to achieve your goal, the more intense will be your desire. Reasons are the fuel in the furnace of achievement.

If you have one or two reasons for attaining a goal, you will have a small amount of motivation. But if you have forty or fifty reasons for achieving a particular goal, you will be so motivated and determined to succeed that nothing and no one will stand in your way.

I have had friends over the years who decided that they wanted to make a lot of money and achieve financial independence. They then wrote out lists of literally hundreds of things that they would do with the money that they intended to earn and accumulate. These people, each in their own areas, became extraordinarily successful far faster than could have been predicted because they had so many reasons for achieving their goals. The more reasons you can think of, the more intense will be your desire and the deeper will be your belief and your conviction that your goal is attainable.

Practice Blue-Sky Thinking

In Charles Garfield's studies of "peak performers," he made an interesting discovery. He analyzed men and women who had achieved only average results at work for many years but who suddenly exploded into great success and accomplishment. He found that at the "take-off point," every one of them began engaging in what he called "blue-sky thinking."

In blue-sky thinking, you imagine that all things are possible for you, just like looking up into a clear blue sky with no limits. You project forward several years and imagine that your life is perfect in every respect.

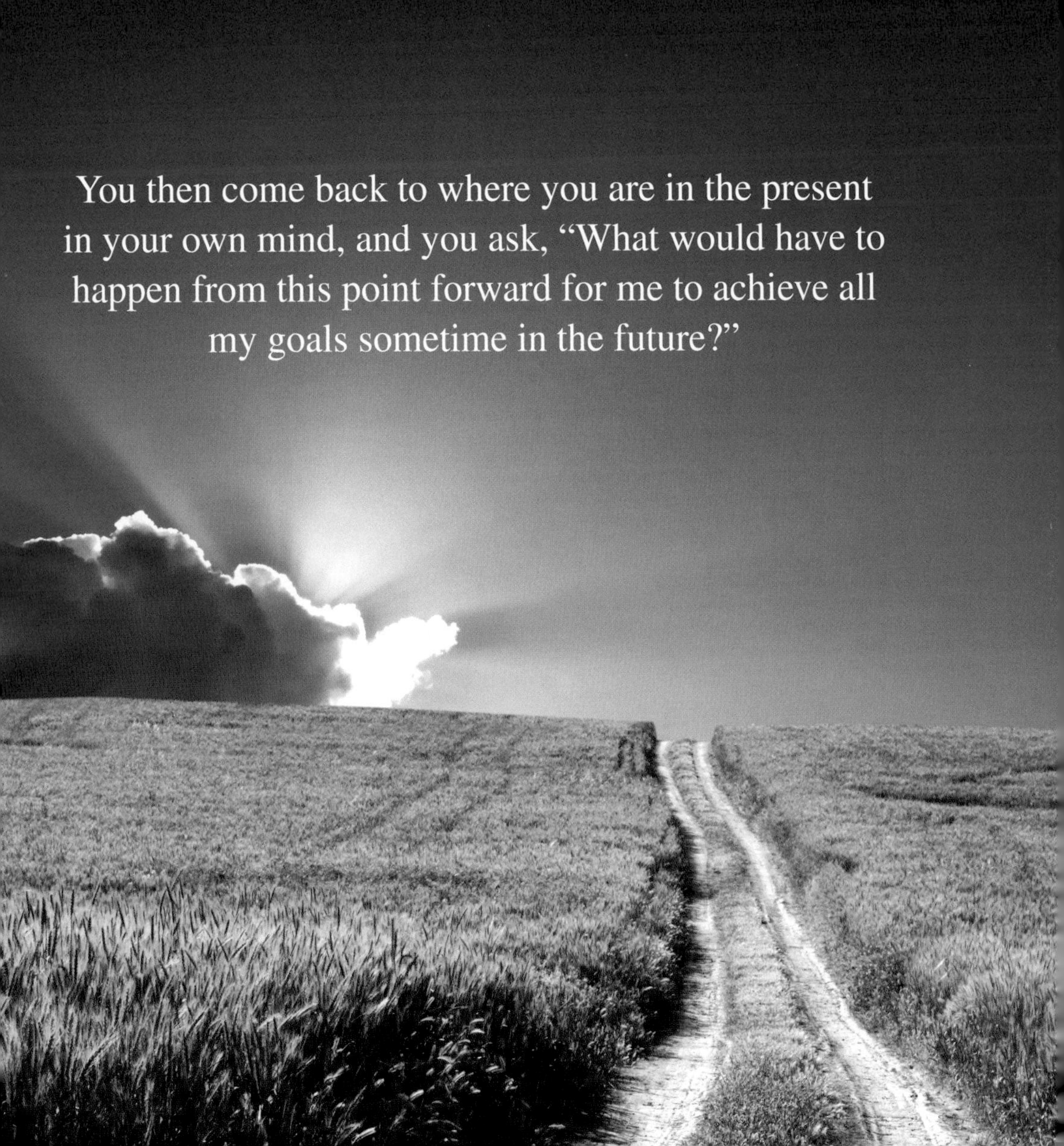

You then come back to where you are in the present in your own mind, and you ask, "What would have to happen from this point forward for me to achieve all my goals sometime in the future?"

Create Your Ideal Future

Remember that "happiness is the progressive realization of a worthy ideal." When you have clear, exciting goals and ideals, you will feel happier about yourself and your world. You will be more positive and optimistic. You will feel internally motivated to get up and get going every morning because every step you are taking will be moving you in the direction of something that is important to you.

Resolve to think about your ideal future most of the time. Remember, the very best days of your life lie ahead. The happiest moments you will ever experience are still to come. The highest income you will ever earn is going to materialize in the months and years ahead. The future is going to be better than anything that may have happened in your past. There are no limits.

The clearer you can be about your long-term future, the more rapidly you will attract people and circumstances into your life to help make that future a reality. The greater clarity you have about who you are and what you want, the more you will achieve and the faster you will achieve it in every area of your life.

6

Set a Deadline

Step number six is for you to set a deadline for the achievement of your goal. A deadline is a "best guess" of when you will attain the goal. It is like aiming at a target. You may hit the bull's-eye, or you may hit to one side or the other. You will achieve fully half of the goals that you set for yourself before your deadline, and you will probably achieve half of your goals after the deadline. But you must have a deadline, just like a scheduled departure time for an airline flight, whether or not it leaves on the particular minute written on your boarding card.

If your goal is big enough, break your deadline down into sub-deadlines. This can be very helpful. I worked with a company recently that had hired a young MBA into the sales department. This young man had taken courses on financial analysis and planning. He therefore wrote down his sales goals by the year, by the month, by the week, and even by the day. He analyzed his activities and compared them against his goals every day, sometimes twice a day. Within six months of starting, he was the most successful salesman in his company. His sales increased steadily and predictably month after month. When you break your goals down into daily and hourly amounts and activities, you will be astonished at how much more you get done.

Three Keys to Peak Performance

The three keys to peak performance in achieving your goals are commitment, completion, and closure.

Commitment

When you make a firm commitment to achieve a particular goal, and you put aside all excuses, it is very much like stepping on the accelerator of your subconscious mind. You will be more creative, determined, and focused than ever before. Great men and women are those who make clear, unequivocal commitments and then refuse to budge from them, no matter what happens.

Completion

Completion is the second ingredient in peak performance. There is an enormous difference between doing 95 percent of a task and doing 100 percent of a task. In fact, it is very common for people to work very hard up to the 90 percent or 95 percent level and then slack off and delay the final completion of the task. This is a temptation that you must fight against. You must continually force yourself, discipline yourself, to resist this natural tendency and push through to completion.

Close the Loop

The third C, after commitment and completion, is closure. This is the difference between an "open loop" and a "closed loop." Bringing closure to an issue in your personal or business life is absolutely essential for you to feel happy and in control of your situation.

Lack of closure—unfinished business, an incomplete action of any kind—is a major source of stress, dissatisfaction, and even failure in business. It consumes enormous amounts of physical and emotional energy.

Set the Target

Remember, you can't hit a target that you can't see. The greater the clarity you have with regard to deadlines and measures, the more you will accomplish and the faster you will get it done.

A goal or a decision without a deadline is merely a wish. It has no energy behind it. It is like a bullet with no powder in the cartridge. Unless you establish deadlines to which you are committed, you will end up "firing blanks" in life and work. Sometimes people ask, "What if I set a deadline and I don't achieve the goal by the deadline?"

Simple. Set another deadline and then another, if necessary. Deadlines are "best-guess" estimates of when a task will be completed. The more you set and work toward deadlines, the more accurate you will become in predicting the time necessary to complete them. You will become better and better at achieving your goals and completing your tasks on schedule every time.

If You Measure It, You Can Manage It

In each area of your life, analyze your activities carefully and select a specific number that, more than anything else, determines your level of success in that area. Then focus all of your attention, all day long, on that specific number. The very act of focused attention will cause you to perform better in that area, both consciously and unconsciously.

If you want to be healthier, you could focus on the number of minutes per week that you exercise or the number of calories per day that you eat. If you want to be successful financially, you could focus on the amount you earn each hour or the amount that you save each month. If you want to be successful in sales, you could focus on the number of calls you make each day or the number of sales or the size of the sales you make each month. If you want to be successful in your relationships, you could focus on the number of minutes that you spend face to face with the most important people in your life each day and each week.

You have heard the saying "What gets measured gets done." There is another saying: "If you can't measure it, you can't manage it." Your ability to set specific measures on your goals, keep an accurate record, and track your performance each day will help ensure that you achieve your goals exactly when you have decided to—or even before.

7

Identify the Obstacles in Your Way

The seventh step in goal setting is for you to determine the obstacles that are standing between you and your goal. Why aren't you at your goal already? What is blocking you? What is holding you back? Of all the things that are holding you back from attaining your goal, what is the biggest, single obstacle?

You can apply the 80/20 Rule to the obstacles and difficulties blocking you from achieving your goals. This rule says that, in most cases, 80 percent of the reasons you are not attaining your goals are internal. They are within you rather than in the world around you. Only 20 percent of the obstacles are contained in your external situation or in other people.

Average and mediocre people always blame their failures to make progress on the people and circumstances around them. But superior people always look into themselves and ask, "What is it in me that is holding me back?"

Think in Terms of Solutions

Remember, you become what you think about most of the time. In the area of problems and difficulties, successful people have a particular way of thinking that we call "solution orientation."

Successful people think about solutions most of the time. Unsuccessful people think about problems and difficulties most of the time. Solution-oriented people are constantly looking for ways to get over, around, and past the obstacles that stand in their way. Problem-oriented people talk continuously about their problems, who or what caused them, how unhappy or angry they are, and how unfortunate it is that these problems have occurred. Solution-oriented people, on the other hand, simply ask the question, "How can we solve this?" They then take action to deal with the problem.

Between you and anything you want to accomplish you will always find problems or obstacles of some kind. This is why success is sometimes defined as the ability to solve problems. Personal leadership is the ability to solve problems. So is effectiveness. All men and women who accomplish anything of importance are people who have developed the ability to solve the problems that stand between them and their goals.

Problem Solving Is a Skill

Fortunately, problem solving is a skill, like riding a bicycle or typing on a keyboard, which you can learn. The more you focus on solutions, the more solutions will come to you. The better you get at solving problems, the faster you will be at solving each subsequent problem. As you get better and faster at solving problems, you will attract even bigger and more expensive problems to solve. Eventually, you will be solving problems that can have significant financial consequences for you and others. This is the way the world works.

The fact is that you have the ability to solve any problem or to overcome any obstacle on the path to your goal if you desire the goal intensely enough. You have within you, right now, all the intelligence and ability you will ever need to overcome any obstacle that could possibly hold you back.

Two Major Obstacles to Success

The two major obstacles to success and achievement are **fear** and **doubt**. It is first of all the fear of failure, poverty, loss, embarrassment, or rejection that holds most people back from trying in the first place. This is why people often give up so easily. As soon as they think of the goal, these fears overwhelm them and, like a bucket of water on a small fire, extinguish their desire completely.

The second mental obstacle, closely aligned to fear, is self-doubt. We doubt our own abilities. We compare ourselves unfavorably to others and think that others are somehow better, smarter, and more competent than we are. We think, "I'm not good enough." We feel inadequate and inferior to the challenges of achieving the great goals that we so much want to accomplish.

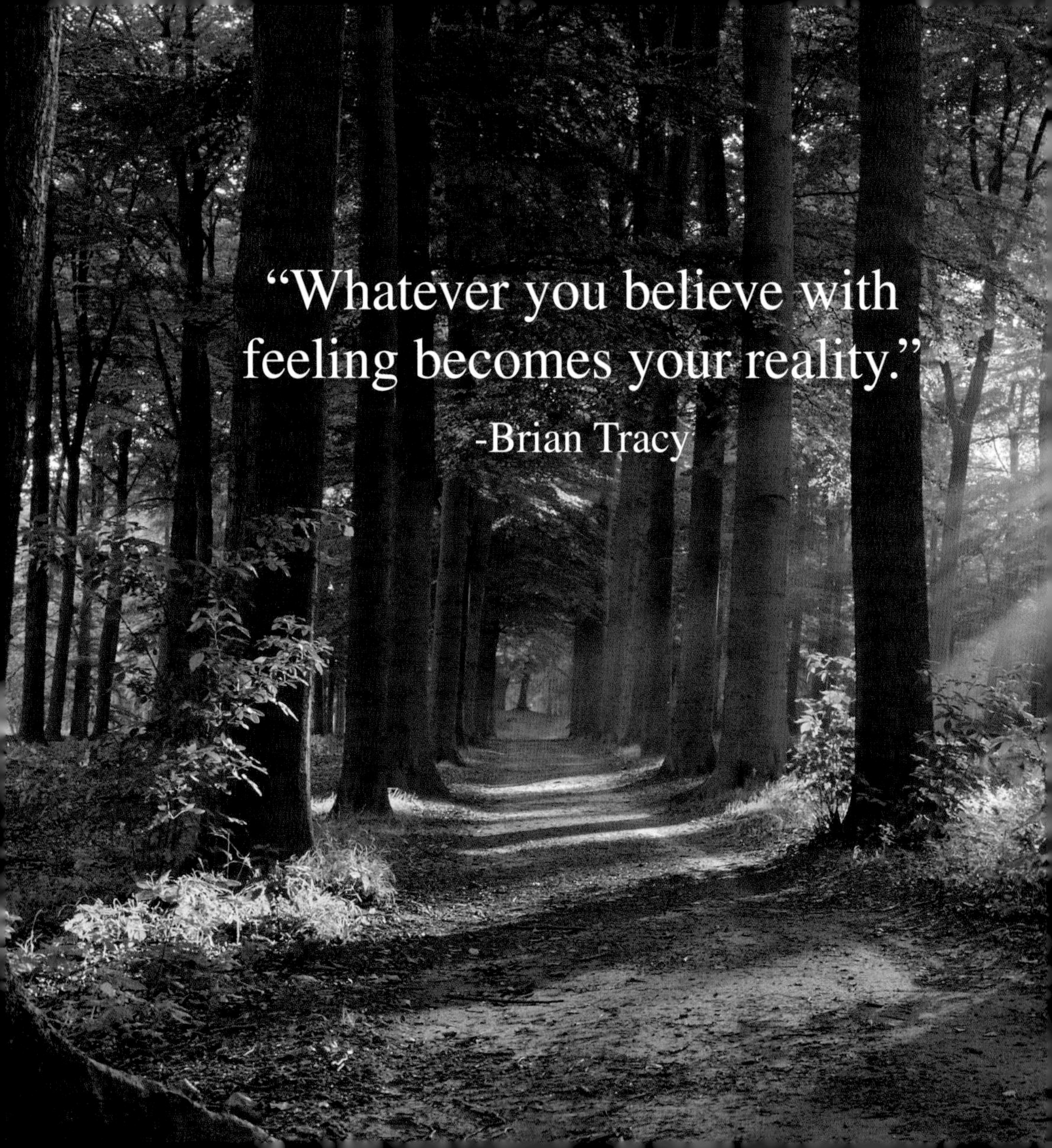
"Whatever you believe with
feeling becomes your reality."
-Brian Tracy

THE KEYS TO COURAGE AND CONFIDENCE

The way that you develop courage and confidence is with knowledge and skill. Most fear and doubt arises out of ignorance and feelings of inadequacy of some kind. The more you learn what you need to know to achieve your goals, the less fear you will feel on the one hand and the more courage and confidence you will feel on the other.

Think about learning to drive for the first time. You were probably extremely tense and nervous and made a lot of mistakes. You may have driven erratically and been a danger to yourself and others. But over time, as you mastered the knowledge and skills of driving, you became better and better and your confidence increased.

Today, you can quite comfortably get into your car and drive across the country with no fear or worry at all. You are so competent at driving that you can do it well without even thinking about it. The same principles apply to any skills you need to learn to achieve any goal you can set for yourself.

Almost Every Problem Can Be Solved

Remember the old poem, "For every problem under the sun, there is a solution or there is none. If there is a solution, go and find it. If there isn't, never mind it."

For every problem or obstacle that is standing between you and what you want to accomplish, there is usually a solution of some kind somewhere. Your job is to be absolutely clear about what sets the speed at which you achieve your goal and then focus your time and attention on alleviating that constraint. By removing your major obstacle, you will often make more progress in a few months than most other people might make in several years.

8

Determine the Additional Knowledge and Skills You Need

Step number eight is for you to *determine the additional knowledge, information, and skills you will require* to achieve your goal. Remember, in the information age, knowledge is the raw material of success. To achieve something you have never achieved before, you will have to do something you have never done before. You will have to become someone you have never been before. To go beyond your current level of accomplishment, you will have to acquire knowledge and skills you have never had before.

Every new goal should be combined with a learning objective. Whatever your goal, you must decide what you will have to learn and master to attain it. Ask yourself, "What one skill, if I developed and did it in an excellent fashion, would help me the most to achieve this goal?" Whatever your answer, you should write it down, make a plan, and then work on developing that skill, every single day, until you master it. This decision alone could change your life.

One Skill Away

Here is the rule: You could be only one skill away from doubling your productivity, performance, and income. You may only need to bring up your skill level in one area for you to be able to use all of your other skills at a higher level. Remember that all skills are learnable. They are not genetically determined. If you need to learn any skill to realize and utilize your full potential, you can learn it by practice and repetition.

Excellence Is a Journey

There is an old saying: "Anything worth doing well is worth doing poorly at first." It is not practice that makes perfect; it is imperfect practice that eventually makes perfect.

Whenever you start something new, you can expect to do it poorly. You will feel clumsy and awkward at first. You will feel inadequate and inferior. You will often feel silly and embarrassed. But this is the price that you pay to achieve excellence in your field. You will always have to pay the price of success, and that price often involves the hard work of mastering a difficult skill that you need to move to the top of your field.

The Three-Plus-One Formula

The three-plus-one formula for mastering any skill is simple, and it works every single time.

First, read in the skill area each day, even if only for fifteen to thirty minutes. Knowledge is cumulative. The more you read and learn, the more confident you will become that you can do this job in an excellent fashion.

Second, listen to educational audio programs on the subject in your car. Average drivers today spend five hundred to one thousand hours each year in their cars driving around during the day. Turn driving time into learning time. You can become one of the best educated people in your field by simply listening to audio programs in your car rather than music.

Third, attend seminars and workshops on your subject. Many people's lives have been changed completely by attendance at a single one- or two-day seminar on a key subject. Forever after, they were completely different in that area.

And the final factor is to practice what you learn at the earliest possible opportunity. Every time you hear a good idea, take action on it. The person who hears one idea and takes action on it is more valuable than a person who hears a hundred ideas but takes action on none of them.

Practice, Practice, Practice

Resolve today, right now, to join the top 10 percent of people in your field. Determine who they are, what they earn, and what they do differently from you. Determine the special knowledge and skills they have developed and resolve to develop them yourself. Remember, anything that anyone has done, within reason, you can do as well. No one is better than

you and no one is smarter than you. The very fact that the top people in your field were at one time not even in your field at all is proof that whatever they have achieved, you can achieve yourself if you simply set it as a goal and work at it long enough and hard enough. There are no limits.

9

Determine the People Whose Help You Will Need

Step number nine is for you to determine the people whose cooperation and assistance you will need to achieve your goal. Everything in life and business is relationships. Everything you accomplish or fail to accomplish will be bound up with other people in some way. Your ability to form the right relationships with the right people at every stage of your life and career will be the critical determinant of your success and achievement and will have an inordinate impact on how quickly you achieve your goals.

The more people you know, and who know you in a positive way, the more successful you will be at anything you attempt. One person, at the right time, in the right place, can open a door for you that can change your life and save you years of hard work.

Get Around the Right People

Make it a point to associate with the kind of people that you like, admire, respect, and want to be like sometime in the future. Associate with the kind of people that you look up to and would be proud to introduce to your friends and associates. The choice of a positive, goal-oriented reference group can do more to supercharge your career than any other factor.

Your Most Important Relationships

We all need the support of family and friends. It is vital that you invest all the time and emotion necessary to build and maintain a high-quality home life. When your family life is solid and secure, characterized by warm, loving relationships, you will do better in everything else in the outer world.

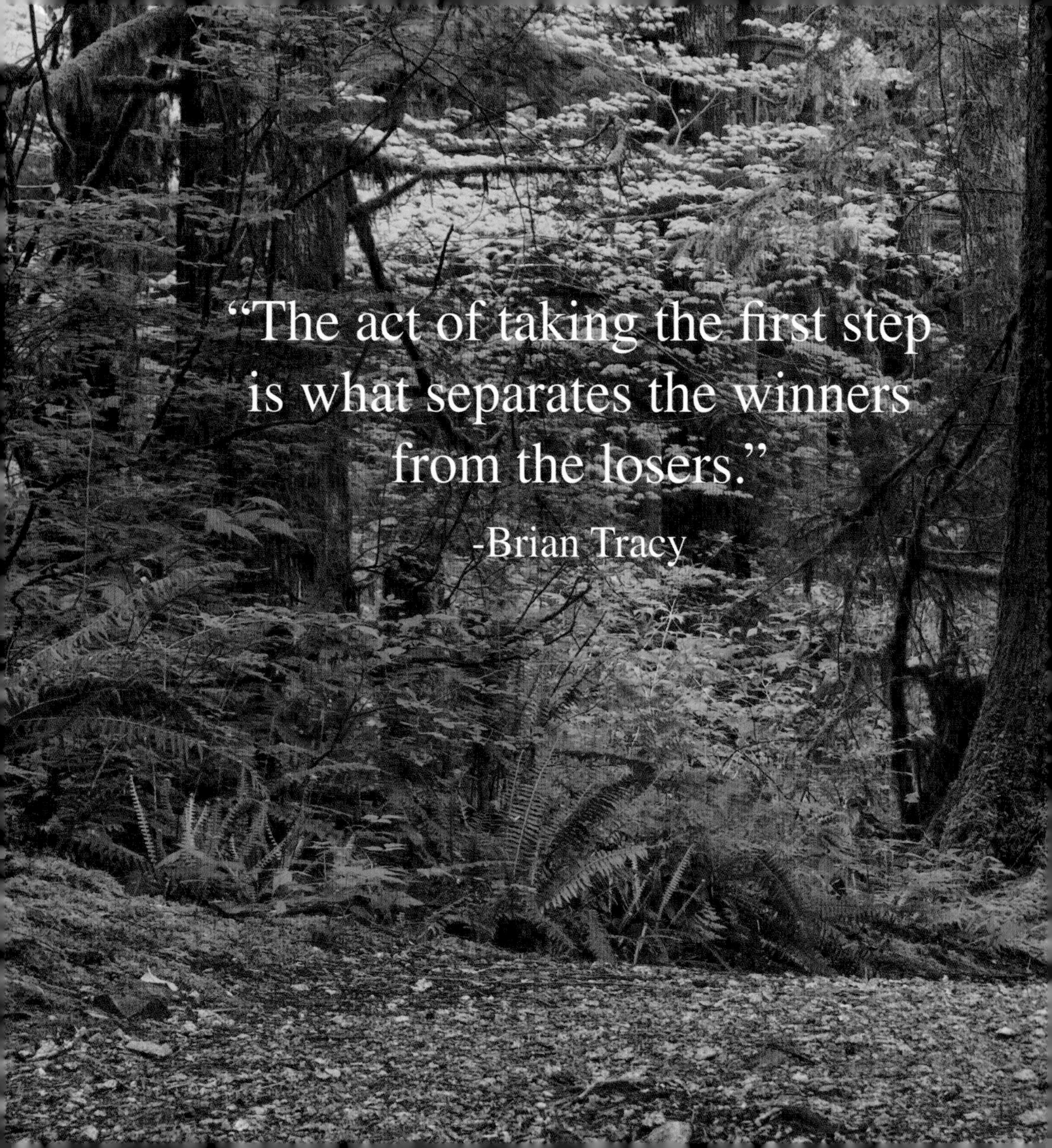
"The act of taking the first step
is what separates the winners
from the losers."
-Brian Tracy

Become a Relationship Expert

Once you have decided upon the people, groups, and organizations whose help and cooperation you will need to achieve your goals, resolve to become a relationship expert. Always treat people with kindness, courtesy, and compassion. Practice the Golden Rule: **Do unto others as you would have them do unto you.**

Above all, the simplest strategy is to treat everyone you meet, at home or at work, like a "million-dollar customer."

Treat other people as though they are the most important people in the world. Treat them as though they were capable of buying a million dollars worth of your product or service. Every day, in every way, look for ways to lighten the load and help other people to do their jobs better and live their lives more easily. This will build up a great reservoir of positive feeling toward you that will come back to benefit you year after year.

10

Make A Plan. Put it all Together

Your ability to set goals and make plans for their accomplishment is the "master skill of success." No other skill will help you more in fulfilling your potential in achieving everything that you are able to accomplish.

All major accomplishments today are "multi-task jobs." They consist of a series of steps that must be taken in a particular way in order to accomplish a result of any significance. Even something as simple as preparing a dish in the kitchen with a recipe is a multi-task job. Your ability to master the skill of planning and completing multi-task jobs will enable you to accomplish vastly more than most people and is critical to your success.

The purpose of planning is to enable you to turn your major definite purpose into a planned, multi-tasked project with specific steps—a beginning, middle, and end—with clear deadlines and sub-deadlines. Fortunately, this is a skill that you can learn and master with practice. This skill will make you one of the most effective and influential people in your business or organization, and the more you practice it, the better you will get at it.

The Basis of All Great Achievements

Every minute spent in planning saves ten minutes in execution. Every minute that you spend planning and thinking before you begin will save you time, money, and energy in getting the results you desire. This is why it is said that "failing to plan is planning to fail." In fact, Proper Prior Planning Prevents Poor Performance.

Here are some suggestions for proper planning:

- List every task and activity
- Determine priority and sequence
- Identify the vital elements of a plan and focus on those
- Expect failure at first
- Focus on the solution
- Revisit and revise your plan regularly

"Excellence/Perfection is not a
destination; it is a continuous
journey that never ends."
-Brian Tracy

Planning Is the Key to Success

The good news is that the very act of planning improves and streamlines the entire process of goal achievement. The better you get at planning, the more ideas and opportunities you will attract to you to plan and achieve even bigger and better things.

Your ability to decide exactly what you want, write it down, make a plan, and then execute that plan is the key to personal effectiveness and high achievement. These are learnable skills that you can master. In no time at all, you can transform your life or business, double your sales or profitability, achieve your goals, and fulfill your true potential.

Manage Your Time Well

To achieve all your goals and become everything you are capable of becoming, you must get your time under control.

Here are some suggestions:

1. Make a list of everything you would like to be, do, or have in the months and years ahead. Analyze your list and select those items that can have the greatest possible consequences on your life.

2. The evening before, make a list of everything you have to do the next day. Let your subconscious mind work on your list while you sleep.

3. Organize your list by priority. Separate the urgent from the non-urgent and the important from the non-important before you begin.

4. Select the most important task, the one with the greatest possible consequences for completion or non-completion, and circle it, making it your A-1 job.

5. Begin working immediately on your most important task, and then discipline yourself to concentrate single-mindedly on this one task until it is 100 percent complete.

Develop the Habits of Time Management

One rule for success is this: Develop good habits and make them your masters.

Whenever you find yourself slowing down or experiencing the urge to procrastinate or delay, repeat to yourself, "Do it now! Do it now! Do it now!" Develop a sense of urgency. Create a bias for action. Get started, get going, and work fast. Discipline yourself to select your most important task, launch into it immediately, and then stay with it until it is done. These time-management practices are the keys to peak performance in every part of your life.

11

Visualize Your Goal Continuously

Step number eleven in goal setting is for you to visualize your goal each day as if it were already attained. See your goal vividly in your mind's eye. Imagine what it would look like if you had already accomplished it. Get the feeling that you would have if you were at your goal already. Imagine the pride, satisfaction, and happiness you would experience if you were already the person you wanted to be, with the goal that you want to enjoy.

Repeat this visualization, combined with the feeling that goes with it, over and over during the day. Each time that you visualize and emotionalize, you program your goal deeper and deeper into your subconscious and superconscious minds. Eventually, your goal becomes a powerful unconscious force motivating and inspiring you day and night.

Feed Your Mind with Exciting Images

Your performance on the outside is always consistent with your self-image on the inside. Your self-image is made up of the mental pictures that you feed into your mind prior to any event. And the good news is that you have complete control over your mental pictures for good or for ill. You can choose to feed your mind with positive, exciting success images, or you can, by default, allow yourself to be preoccupied by failure images. The choice is up to you.

Almost everything that you have achieved in life, or failed to achieve, is the result of the use or misuse of visualization. If you look back, you will find that almost everything you visualized positively eventually came true for you. You visualized completing school, and you did it. You visualized getting your first car, and you got it. You visualized your first romance or relationship, and you met the right person. You visualized taking a trip, getting a job, finding an apartment, or purchasing certain clothes, and all these events came true for you.

Two Ways to Stimulate Your Superconscious Mind

There are two ways for you to stimulate your superconscious mind into action. The first is for you to concentrate and work intensely on achieving your goal. Throw your whole heart into what you are doing. Think about it, talk about it, write it, rewrite it, and review it every single day. Do everything that you can possibly think of that can help you to attain that goal.

When you dedicate yourself to continuous, determined forward action toward the accomplishment of your goal, all sorts of serendipitous and synchronous events will happen to you and for you. People will emerge from unexpected places to help you. You will receive phone calls and offers of assistance. You will come across ideas and information that you would not have recognized before. You will have ideas and insights that move you even faster toward your goal.

The second way to stimulate your superconscious mind is to relax completely and get your mind busy elsewhere. For example, when you go on vacation, you often become so busy with other activities that you don't think about your goals or problems at all. It seems that the more you can completely relax and let go, both mentally and physically, the more rapidly your superconscious mind will click into action and begin giving you the ideas and insights that you need. In other words, the harder that you "don't try," the faster your superconscious mind will work for you.

You should try both methods on every goal. First, work with single-minded concentration on the goal. Commit 100 percent of your energies to solving the problem. Then, if you have still not experienced the breakthrough you desire, get your mind busy elsewhere. Take some time off. Go on vacation. Engage in physical exercise or go to a movie. Forget about your goal completely for a while. Then, at exactly the right time, your superconscious mind will function and the answer will appear.

The Beginning of All Improvement

All improvement in your life starts with an improvement in your mental pictures. Start today to flood your mind with pictures of the person you want to be, the life you want to live, and the goals you want to achieve. Cut out pictures from magazines and newspapers that are consistent with your goals and desires. Post them everywhere. Review them regularly. Discuss them often. Imagine them continually.

Make your life an ongoing process of positive visualization, continually imagining and "visioneering" your ideal goals and your perfect future. This can do more to help you to step on the accelerator of your own potential than any other exercise you engage in.

12

Never Give Up

Finally, the twelfth step to goal setting is to back everything you do with persistence and determination. Resolve in advance that you will never give up. Make the decision, long before you face any obstacles or difficulties, that no matter what happens, you will persevere until you finally reach your goal.

This form of mental preparation, deciding in advance that you will never give up, can do more to help you than almost any other factor. You will encounter many setbacks and disappointments on the way to your goal. This is inevitable and unavoidable. It goes with the territory. You must decide, in advance, that nothing will stop you. Then, when you face the inevitable obstacles and difficulties that occur, you will be psychologically prepared. You will bounce rather than break.

Self-Discipline Is the Core Quality

The single most important quality for success is self-discipline. Self-discipline means that you have the ability, within yourself, based on your strength of character and willpower, to do what you should do, when you should do it, whether you feel like it or not.

Character is the ability to follow through on a resolution after the enthusiasm with which the resolution was made has passed. It is not what you learn that is decisive for your future. It is whether or not you can discipline yourself to pay the price, over and over, until you finally obtain your objective.

You need self-discipline in order to set your goals and to make plans for their accomplishment. You need self-discipline to continually revise and upgrade your plans with new information. You need self-discipline to use your time well and to always concentrate on the one most important task that you need to do at the moment. You need self-discipline to invest in yourself every day, to build yourself up personally and professionally, to learn what you need to learn in order to enjoy the success of which you are capable.

No matter how well you organize yourself and your activities, you will experience countless disappointments, setbacks, obstacles, and adversity over the course of your life. And the higher and more challenging the goals you set for yourself, the more disappointment and adversity you will experience.

This is the paradox. It is impossible for us to evolve, grow, and develop to our full potential unless we face adversity and learn from it. All of the great lessons of life come as the result of setbacks and temporary defeats, which we have done our utmost to avoid. Adversity therefore comes unbidden in spite of our best efforts. And yet without it, we cannot grow into the kind of people who are capable of scaling the heights and achieving great goals.

Conclusion

You have now learned perhaps the most comprehensive strategy for setting and achieving goals that has ever been put together in one book. By practicing these rules and principles, you can accomplish more in the coming months and years than most people accomplish in a lifetime.

The most important quality you can develop for lifelong success is the habit of taking action on your plans, goals, ideas, and insights. The more often you try, the sooner you will triumph. There is a direct relationship between the number of things you attempt and your accomplishments in life.

These are the steps for setting and achieving goals and for living an extraordinary life. **Nothing can stop you now**.

About the Author

Brian Tracy is one of the top professional speakers and trainers in the world today. He addresses more than 250,000 men and women each year on the subjects of leadership, strategy, sales, and personal and business success. He has given more than five thousand talks and seminars to five million people throughout the United States, Canada, and worldwide.

Brian is an avid student of business, psychology, management, sales, history, economics, politics, metaphysics, and religion. He brings a unique blend of humor, insight, information, and inspiration to the more than one hundred talks and seminars he conducts worldwide each year. Brian believes that each person has extraordinary untapped potential that he or she can learn to access and, in so doing, accomplish more in a few years than the average person does in a lifetime.

Brian Tracy is the chairman of Brian Tracy International, a human resource development company headquartered in Solana Beach, California. He has written fifty books and produced more than four hundred audio and video training programs. His materials have been translated into thirty-six languages and are used in fifty-four countries.

Brian lives with his wife, Barbara, and their four children in Solana Beach, California. He is active in community affairs and serves as a consultant to several nonprofit organizations.

If you have enjoyed this book we invite you to check out our entire collection of gift books, with free inspirational movies, at

www.simpletruths.com

You'll discover it's a great way to inspire friends and family, or to thank your best customers and employees.

For more information, please visit us at:

www.simpletruths.com or call us toll free... 800-900-3427